# Access to His Grace

*I loved her but didn't want her.*

# Kentavia Johnson

Access to His Grace © 2022 by Kentavia Johnson. All Rights Reserved.

All rights reserved. No part of this book may be reproduced in any form or by any electronic or mechanical means including information storage and retrieval systems, without permission in writing from the author. The only exception is by a reviewer, who may quote short excerpts in a review.

The Holy Bible, New International Version®, NIV® Copyright © 1973, 1978, 1984, 2011 by Biblica, Inc.® Used by permission. All rights reserved worldwide.

Cover designed by AviLuxe Designs

Visit the author's website at www.kentaviaj.com.

Printed in the United States of America
First Printing: January 2022
The Scribe Tribe Publishing Group

ISBN-978-1-7376411-2-4 (print)
ISBN – 978-1-7376411-3-1 (ebook)

*In memory of Lanetta Smith (Jesus' Best Friend, Best Friend), who didn't judge me. She looked past my sin and saw a young woman who was hurting on the inside, feeling lonely and misunderstood without a voice. She encouraged me with the simple, but secure words, "Drop her off to me when you feel it's too much." I have never ever forgotten those words. They meant so much to me.*
*I love you, Lanetta!*

*To my daughter, Zharia:*

*I didn't know what to do with you.*
*I didn't pray for you while you were in the womb.*
*I didn't sing to you, and I didn't read to you.*
*But you are God's grace.*
*I should've named you God's grace because God showed me grace when He chose me to be your mom.*
*You're kind, smart, wise, witty, respectful.*
*And all because of God's grace.*
*I carried you with shame, hurt, anger, disconnection, and sadness, not knowing that God's grace shielded you from it all.*
*You came out loving me more than I loved you.*
*Never resentful but gracious.*
*Loving, never hateful.*
*Mature while I was still immature.*
*You waited on me fervently. Having faith that I would be the mom you needed me to be.*
*You had more faith in me than I had in myself.*
*Some days I still wonder if I've failed you, but you love me beyond my faults, my guilt trips, and my immaturity.*
*You love me for me.*
*You listen to me.*
*You respect me.*
*You trust me.*

*I love you so much.*
*I pray every day that you feel my love,*
*And never doubt my love for you.*
*I know that God has a special plan for you! Because He kept you.*
*Keep Him first, my flower princess, and let God guide your footsteps.*

*You were meant to be here. I was so blinded by guilt, shame, and disappointment that I could not see my blessing and the grace of God. I had no idea that my story, my journey, our journey would be my healing and my encouragement to the world. Thank you for helping me discover that I have full Access to His Grace.*

# Acknowledgements

To anyone who has struggled to forgive yourself, bound by disappointment, shame, guilt, and embarrassment, I'm here to tell you that you can and will make it! You have *Access to His Grace*. God showed me grace and He loves you equally. He has the same grace waiting for you. Just trust Him.

To Neesha: I swear your voice changed that day when you said with all confidence, "When are you gonna stop being scared and grab your microphone?" I thought when someone prophesied to me it would be a clear statement like, "You're getting married in 2021." or "God said you will receive that new job this year." What microphone?! I was too confused. I was secretly hoping for, "Your good husband is coming!" But Neesha, here we are. I'm on the mic!

To Pastor John F. Hannah and New Life Covenant Church SE: As I searched for places to worship and heal, I journeyed through different churches in search of "the right one." Being that I attended my family childhood church all my life and I was attached, I wanted to make sure that when I made the decision to join another church it was the right decision. Not just for me but for my baby. 13 years later and I have never looked back.

*~Access to His Grace~*

# Contents

Foreword ~ 7
Where's My Family Unit? ~ 9
Operation Hide This Baby ~ 15
Not So Solid Plan ~ 27
Plan B ~ 33
Church Girls Apologize ~ 39
Don't Shower Me ~ 45
Why Do Women Do This? ~ 46
Medicating The Pain Of My Guilt ~ 53
It's Not Your Fault, Baby ~ 63
Access To His Grace ~ 67
It's Available To You ~ 73
Mother-Daughter Activity ~ 77

*~Access to His Grace~*

# Foreword

I will never forget the time my mom and I first had "the conversation" and not *that* conversation. The conversation about my mother's journey with me. The one when she told me that she was thinking about aborting me. I wasn't upset or sad because I understood. I understood that her life would've changed drastically. I understood she was young, and her life had just begun. I understood she wasn't ready for a child mentally and financially.

Every kid's dream is to grow up in a two-parent home and have that big family experience but being that friend that grows up in a single parent home, you start to compare your home life with the others around you. That was me. I compared my home life with my friends and questioned what my life would be like if this or that was different. Even though God didn't see fit for me to grow up in a two-parent family home, I wouldn't trade our story for anything. Despite not growing up with my dad in the home, I still experienced the right amount of love, attention, affirmations, and spiritual guidance. That alone means my mom did an amazing job and she continues to do so.

~Zharia Aianna

**For it is by grace you have been saved, through faith—and this is not from yourselves, it is the gift of God.**

**—Ephesians 2:8**

# Where's My Family Unit?

I am a single mom. I AM A SINGLE MOM. I've never written those words before on paper. I've rarely even uttered those five words unless I used it in a joking manner with my friends.

Raise *your* hand if you want to be a single mom? I don't think anyone ever says, "Yea, when I grow up, imma be a single mama!" And let me tell you, I certainly didn't. I grew up watching my mom do it by herself. She didn't complain about being a single mother, but I knew in my heart she couldn't have possibly pictured her life as a single mom of two children. I mean, really, who would?

For nine months straight, I cried. I cried and I cried. I never even knew a person could cry that much. How---well, *why* did I get pregnant? I always told myself that I would never ever be a single mom. I didn't pray for a husband, but I definitely didn't pray for a baby daddy! Struggling was not a part of my plan. I refused to be a statistic raising a baby alone. From what I could see, raising a child alone was no easy feat and I desired no parts of that. I wanted a family unit. I deserved the family unit. But a family unit was not in my cards.

My daughter's father and I sat in the abortion clinic on the northside of Chicago waiting for my name to be called. I was the one waiting to have my insides vacuumed out, but he was the one reeking of nervousness.

*"Are you ok?" I asked.*
*"No, I have those things in my stomach."*
*"Butterflies?" I questioned as I rolled my eyes.*
*"Yea, that."*

Welp, I was fine! I was just ready to get it over with! Anxiety nor fear had a place in my feelings. Instead, I was excited. To know that I was about to get that thing out of me and move on with my regularly scheduled program brought nothing but joy to my soul!

I glanced around the room as I patiently waited for my name to be called. As my eyes scanned the surroundings, I noticed a Caucasian lady with blonde hair. She looked to be about 30ish or maybe she was really 20 and just lived a hard knock life. I wasn't sure, but she had my attention. She was calm and cool. Her body language read, *"I'm good."*

My conclusion was either she'd had an abortion before, or she was there to get a routine check-up. Either way, I didn't want to be *that* calm and cool like getting an abortion was the same as my weekly manicure. Yet, I also refused to punk out, so I suppressed any rising fear.

Finally, my name was called. I went back to the examination room where there was eerily dim lighting. As I reflect now, it was spooky, but I did not care then. I was on a mission. I climbed on the table as an emotionless, Black woman gave me an examination. I guess with her type of job, emotions had to be left at home. Who goes to an abortion clinic for attachment? I don't remember a lot of eye contact between the two of us and the machine was turned away so I couldn't see the fetus. I'm sure that was purposeful. She placed a condom on the transducer, inserted it and began her examination. She asked when my last period was. I told her, "back in March sometime." Once her examination was complete, she explained to me that I was much further along than I thought. In such an uncaring voice, she added, "You'll have to come back."

I didn't understand. I was so confused. Come back? The hell I would! I was not leaving until it was done! Being further along than I originally thought meant I needed to get it done asap.

I was directed to a counselor who sat behind a glass window and explained my options. My options boiled down to one thing—come back with more money. My savings account would have to be emptied to pay for it. And I knew my mom would kill me if she found out I spent all the money in my savings account. Actually, she would kill me twice. Once for spending the money and again for getting an abortion.

I was devastated. I was confused. I was pissed. How could this happen to me? Everyone else had gotten an abortion. Why couldn't I get one? Why God? Why me? As my daughter's father and I walked out of the clinic, I didn't want to talk. I didn't want to think. I didn't want to think about coming up with a plan B, C, or D. Because plan A should've worked just like it worked for all the other girls I knew who had gotten abortions. I was so confused, but not enough to not be hungry.

My inner fat girl was screaming, probably partly from hunger and the rest from shock. We went to a nearby restaurant where I ordered a burger and fries. As I scarfed down my food, I looked at him and in my most matter-of-factly voice and said, "I'm going to be a single mom."

Of course, he retorted, "No, you're not."

However, I replied softly with even more assurance in my voice and confidence in my heart than the first time I said it.

"Yea...yes I am."

"For I know the plans I have for you," declares the Lord, "plans to prosper you and not to harm you, plans to give you hope and a future."
—Jeremiah 29:11

# Operation Hide This Baby

My greatest wish was to open my eyes and wake from a nightmare. I wanted to wake up on a college campus in my dorm room. In my vision, my new college roommate and I would get dressed and go to a party. But that never happened. I woke up every day as my stomach grew larger and traveled to a city college with my head held down, hoping no one would talk to me. Each day was full of disappointment, guilt, shame and hurt.

I never desired to feel her kick. Even a subtle one would initiate a connection and I refused to bond with the little person growing inside of me. I never even acknowledged I was pregnant. I made no mention of being pregnant if no one else did. I simply moved through my life like nothing was changing when the reality was that my entire world was being shaken up. All I wanted in life was to have a miscarriage and most nights I literally prayed to lose my baby. When it didn't happen on its own, it was clear that my body needed some help, and I was determined to give it the assistance it needed. I had big plans and they did not involve a kid. My plans included stepping into a college dorm room in August, and a baby growing inside of me was counteractive to those plans. Not to mention, it was the summer after my high school graduation and my plan was to live my best life. My friends and I were prepared to kick it hard before we went our separate ways.

In June of that year, my family and I took a family trip to Disney World! I was so excited, not just because I love Disneyworld and it's *the* happiest place on the earth, but also because I knew that one of these "do not get on this ride if you are pregnant" signs would handle my situation with ease and speed. That week in Florida, I rode every roller coaster imaginable. I held my stomach in and proudly walked up to each thriller ride at Universal Studios, Island of Adventure and Disney World. As I stood in line for the Incredible Hulk ride, I was certain that I found the perfect ride to finish the job. I looked up at the roller coaster as it sped around the track at high speed. With its twists and turns, upside-down loops and inside out flips, I was excited to hop on the best ride for anyone who was pregnant and needed a miscarriage. I got on and enjoyed the ride! We continued to rip through Island of Adventure,

and I was like a kid in a candy store. I had the time of my little life! Or at least
tried.

It was easy to hold my stomach in around people, but it was a bit more challenging to hold in my breasts! My breasts were growing by the hour! Now, when I wanted breasts back in high school, I didn't get them, but as a pregnant woman, I looked like Pamela Anderson! I did my best to disguise the girls, but they insisted on making their presence known.

Overall, I had an amazing time at Disney World. My family and I spent time together. We laughed, talked, and bonded over great food, all while I silently prayed for a miscarriage. I never once even considered how a miscarriage really played out. I just thought I'd bleed and that was it. So, that's what I waited for. Blood.
After a week, there was still no blood. Okay, maybe miscarriages don't happen right away. So, I waited another week. Still no blood. I just didn't understand. Why won't this baby just go away? Maybe I was never really pregnant, and it was all in my imagination and my breasts are just finally growing on their own. I decided to take another pregnancy test. Positive! What the hell?!
I had no idea what to do. I was at a loss for words *and* ideas, and I am never without something to say. Without a

job or money, I had no clue how I would get the abortion that I desperately needed.

By the end of July, my belly was poking out a bit more and my breasts were just out of control! I've never been a big breasted girl, so they took more effort to hide. I just continued to hold my stomach in, hoping that no one would notice how big my breasts were getting. I held my stomach in so tight that I didn't give the baby any room to grow.

Scared and confused, I didn't know what I was going to do. I didn't discuss my pregnancy with my daughter's father either. Neither one of us brought it up; he was just as uncomfortable with the pregnancy as I was.

When August arrived, I was excited because I was slated to become a student at Aurora University. My plans for operation abortion were still unclear, but I knew where I would be in late August. I wasn't going too far from home. The school was about an hour away, which was far enough to make me feel like I was away. I was ready! I had my roommate assignment. I had my fridge and my microwave. The baby and I were on our way to college. I still didn't have a big reveal plan but whatever! My hopes were still set high on miscarriage, and I could plan a party to celebrate that. I continued to bombard heaven each night with prayers and pleas for a miscarriage.

Although I still had no plan, it was clear that my godmother had one when she came to our house for her yearly visit from Maryland. I was in the basement, minding my business entertaining my godbrother, who was a year old at the time. My godmother called me upstairs. Initially, I didn't think much of it and just proceeded upstairs with my routine tummy tucked in. The kitchen counter provided support and concealment as I leaned on it and waited to hear what she had to say. She wasted no time!

She blurted out, "You're pregnant. I know you are because your breasts ain't ever been that big." Now, I don't know if she thought that she was doing me a favor, but she could've at least consulted with me first. But we all know when people tell your business, they never seem to consult with you.

Thank you, titties. Thanks very much! I would've been good! But noooooo! My breasts wanted to grow two cup sizes! Well, at that point it was no going back. The jig was up, and it was pointless to lie. I just told the truth.

"Yes, I am."

My truth sent my mom into a disturbing, deep silence. It didn't seem real. It felt like an out-of-body experience. My mom called me into her bedroom where she laid on her back with her eyes closed. The light from the kitchen shone on her face just enough for me to see her expression. She spoke very low and asked me, "How could you do this?" She had no idea that I was just as clueless as she was. I had been asking myself that same question since I found out I was expecting. So, I was not entirely sure how she wanted me to answer that question. I mustered up the only response I could think of.

"I don't know."

What followed my words were the most heartbreaking, devastating words that I hung on to for many years after I first heard them. Very calmly my mother gave me stern directives that would change the course of my life.

"Call the school and tell them you're not coming."

My heart shattered into pieces, and I burst into tears. I left her room and as I headed to return down to the basement, my godmother said, "here take your godbrother. You might as well begin to practice."

I never said a word. I just grabbed my godbrother, took him downstairs with me and sat him on the couch. Repeatedly, I punched my stomach with my fists and silently cried. I cried all night long. And I cried every night for the rest of my pregnancy.

The next day, I didn't call Aurora University. I wasn't ready to accept the fact that my dream was deferred. I also didn't want to accept that I was *still* pregnant. I hadn't thought about the baby growing inside of me much. Hell! My secret was just released after six months of the best magic show I had ever pulled off. On the other hand, my godmother was forging full speed ahead. She had a list of pregnancy to-dos which included finding a prenatal pill and making a doctor's appointment. I didn't want to do any of those things. I didn't want to talk about it, think about it, take a pill, make a doctor's appointment, nothing! I wanted to go away to college! Period.

But nope! My reality was that I was headed to Osco to get some prenatal pills. My godmother wanted to tell me all about how you can get prenatal pills over the counter and blah, blah, blah.

*Who cares?!* I didn't. She bought the prenatal pills and told me I needed to start taking them right away. I was just like, "ok" with the most reassuring face I could put on. I wasn't interested. Next, she made me call the County Hospital to make a prenatal appointment. At that point, she was taking things too far. I needed to draw the line because I was not having a kid at the County. No, thank you. However, I chose not to give any push back because I figured I had caused enough harm. I just held my head down and responded with another soft, "ok."

We called the County and set an appointment for me to go to the doctor to have my first prenatal visit.

It was a long weekend after my official "pregnancy announcement." My big reveal was a far cry from all the elaborate social media announcements with pictures, funny quotes, and themes that we see today. But the secret was out.

I grew up in a two-flat building. My mom and I resided on the first floor and my older sister, my brother-in-law (who I called my brother-dad), my nephew and my soon-to-be niece lived upstairs. The funny thing is that my sister is fifteen years older than me, and our daughters are thirty days apart.

Since we lived in such proximity, we normally crossed paths often. However, that was not the case the weekend of my big reveal. I didn't see my brother-dad or my sister. I think we were all just avoiding each other. It was not confirmed that they already knew, but deep down I felt that the big news had already reached them. We couldn't avoid each other for the rest of our lives, so someone had to say something. My brother-dad did.

After church on Sunday, he called a family meeting. My brother-dad, my sister, my mom, my daughter's father and myself were called to the dining room table. Well, actually, it was my sister and her belly, me and my belly, my mom, my brother-dad, and my daughter's father. My brother-dad did most of the talking. I know he was as disappointed as everyone sitting around the table. Maybe except for my daughter's father because I honestly didn't know how he felt. I never asked because I didn't care. It was my body, my life and my dreams that were halted.

My brother-dad spoke about how he was upset because he had to hear it from my godmother that I was pregnant. Well, that wasn't my fault because it wasn't like I asked her to tell anyone. I didn't ask her to announce my pregnancy; she did that on her own. So, I couldn't be blamed for that. I didn't speak the whole time. I had nothing to say.

My sister expressed how she was very upset with me because I should have told her. *And how was I supposed to do that?* My sister is fifteen years older than me, which means she acted as a mother more than a sister. Now, I love my sister, but she is my *older* sister. The age difference didn't allow us to share sister secrets and stay up at night making tents out of covers and furniture. No, both of us grew up like only children. We had nothing in common really. So, for me to tell my sister would have been the same as telling my mom. So, yea, that wasn't my plan. Sorry, sis.

Interestingly enough, no one asked how I felt. I'm not even sure if anyone cared what I felt, and I dared not attempt to speak up. I loved my brother-dad. He always made me feel safe. He made me laugh and he hardly ever told me "no," nor did he yell at me. He didn't yell that

Sunday either, while he explained to me that everyone would be there to support me through my process.

"*Support me?*" I thought. *Support me how? Please define that!* I couldn't go away to school, and I was one step away from throwing myself down the stairs. How could they support me when they didn't even know exactly what I was feeling?

Before we ended the family meeting. My brother-dad made a suggestion.

"Why don't y'all get married?"

I hadn't said anything the entire time, but that was absurd! It was the right moment for me to speak up. *Hell no! Not I, said Kentavia!*

I calmly replied, "No. That won't be happening."

I looked at Zharia's dad. I am going to be a single parent. I don't want to be with him. This was only a temporary thing. Should I be trying to make this work? Naw, we can't get married. I need to deal with this baby. I can't deal with a husband too! I am not about to ruin my life any further by making a barely boyfriend my husband. I understand your thoughts, brother-dad, but no thank you. That's not happening.

I didn't want to marry my daughter's father. I mean I liked him, but I certainly wasn't in love with him. In my mind, we were going to end our little high school boyfriend-girlfriend thing when I left for college to find a basketball player, get married and live happily ever after! The thought of us continuing in a relationship made me nauseous. Or maybe that was morning sickness? Either way, I didn't want to be with him anymore but since I was pregnant, I figured I at least had to try and make it work a little longer. Anything to keep me from being a single mom.

So no, brother-dad, I do not want to get married. Take that off the table. Thanks for trying to make me an "honest woman," but no thanks. I'll take my chances. When we all left the dining room table, I went to the place where I spent the next four months of my pregnancy--my bedroom. My daughter's father and I tried for a while to do the boyfriend-girlfriend thing, but it just didn't stick. I certainly wasn't surprised though. We were two young teenagers, eighteen and twenty, pretending to love each other and love the fact that we were having a child together. That was entirely too much faking and role-playing.

> "You are my hiding place; you will protect me from trouble and surround me with songs of deliverance."
> —Psalm 32:7

# Not So Solid Plan

On the day of my first appointment, my daughter's father and I went to the wrong hospital! When I set the appointment with my godmother, I thought it was for the County hospital. Because I was too distracted by my own emotions, I never double-checked to confirm. So, we sat in the County Hospital for over three hours waiting to hear my name called. *Now, I heard the County was ridiculous, but geez Louise! Even when you have an appointment too? Good God!* Finally, I went to the receptionist.

"How long does it usually take to be seen by the doctor?"

She shrugged her shoulders and said, "Depends."

*Well, can I get some eye contact?*

I guess not, because she never looked up. I went back to where my daughter's father was seated and told him, "Come on!" I refused to be treated like a second-class citizen. I was furious with the experience, but I was even angrier with myself. I knew exactly what she was thinking.

She figured I was like everyone else who came to the county. I was a black, young chick with minimum education and pregnant. That is what I didn't want. To be stereotyped. I knew that when people saw me, they saw a teenage, pregnant black girl. Everybody does it.

As a society, we are conditioned to judge and label pregnant teenagers. No one ever says anything about the boy who got the girl pregnant. Yet, we needed the boy to even get pregnant. It's always, "she's too stupid" or "she should be ashamed of herself." Or my favorite, "Now why would she do that to herself?" My answer was, I didn't know.

Well, news of my pregnancy spread fast! My growing belly, breasts, and nose were all telltale signs. Of course, as soon as people found out, their slick comments followed. Most times, I had no retort for their rude remarks; I simply sarcastically responded in my mind.

A snide comment was made by someone who I never thought would remark in that manner. "I can't believe you. I can't believe you got yourself pregnant." *Well, it's shocking to me too, if you care to know.* But she didn't care. I know because she just walked off like she had to take care of my baby.

A family member said, "Yea see, Aunt Hattie has this and that to say about other people. Bet she didn't expect you to be pregnant." *Well, I am sure she didn't, but I don't remember my mama making slick remarks about other people being pregnant including you.*

As my belly continued to grow, I mostly kept to myself. I didn't allow people to rub on my stomach and I didn't talk to people. The only exception was that most devastating and embarrassing phone call to Aurora University to tell them I needed to withdraw my admissions. A little more of me died inside after that call. It was such a difficult conversation. The admissions counselor was trying to understand why I needed to withdraw. I just told her that I needed to. I was hoping that she'd get the hint and just say, "Ok. Goodbye, have a nice life." But of course, she didn't. She asked me "why" again with concern and then with some hesitation she probed with the big question.

"Are you pregnant?"

Silence for a moment.

"Yes." I could barely utter that word.

She then said something that gave me a sliver of excitement and hope.

"That's ok. I have a young lady from Chicago who has a baby. She attends during the week and goes home on the weekend. I can give her your number so you can talk to her. Maybe she can change your mind. Would you like that?"

"Yes! I screamed. That time with evident excitement and a little hope in my heart. *Maybe this will change my mother's mind and let me go!* I didn't tell my mom right away. For starters, she wasn't really speaking to me and, two, I wanted to get all the details and then bring her in on the master plan.

The young lady called me the next day with such enthusiasm! She explained her situation and discussed how her baby stayed with her mom during the week and on the weekends, she went home to be with the baby. It was the best decision for her, and she convinced me that it could work for me too.

*Yea! This can work. Aurora is only an hour away. That's nothing! This can work and then next year, my baby can return with me when I can get an apartment off campus.* It sounded like a solid plan, and I was confident that I could work it out. I eagerly shared the plan with my mother, but clearly, she didn't think it was as solid as I thought.

"No, you can't go." It was as cold and stern as the first time she said it.

She didn't even think about it. Nor did she give me an opportunity to explain or try and work with me. It was so unfair! I wanted to yell, "I hate you!" But I didn't. The truth was, I hated myself more than I hated her.

> **I consider that our present sufferings are not worth comparing with the glory that will be revealed in us.**
> **—Romans 8:18**

# Plan B

After the bottom fell out of my initial plan, I sucked it up and enrolled in Harold Washington Community College. I absolutely hated it and I'm sure my face shared how I was feeling. In all my classes, I hid in the back of the room. I went to class and went back home.

I spent my time at school Monday through Friday. On Sundays, I went to church. At home, I maintained my routine for the most part. I ate grilled cheese sandwiches with a side of applesauce and retreated to my bedroom, where I spent most of my pregnant days. All I wanted was for the pregnancy to be over.

But God is amazing. Even amid our valleys, He sends you a sign to remind you that He didn't promise us that every day would be a sunny day. He just made a promise to always be there.

When I was eight months into my pregnancy, I decided to get a part-time job. I figured if the kid was here to stay then surely she would need clothes, pampers and other things that babies required. Honestly, I didn't have a lot of insight into what kids needed. I knew the basics (food, water, clothes, and shelter), but I didn't understand that to be a *good* parent, kids also need your sacrifice, spiritual and moral guidance, consistency and so much more. Kids are expensive physically and mentally!

I applied at Marshall Field's department store, and to my surprise I was hired. It was my first retail job, and it wasn't my cup of tea. I preferred to hear, "Are you finding everything ok, ma'am," not *me* asking the question. Some days I would hide in the dressing room and come out like I had been straightening up the dressing room. I was fat and too tired to be standing on my feet for hours at a time and again, I really didn't want to talk to people. Because then the questions would start. "Oh, how many months are you?" "What are you having? Boy or girl?" "How exciting!" *Exciting for who? Not me.*

Thankfully, I had a cool supervisor who didn't micromanage. I'm sure it's no surprise, but I didn't want her to say much to me and she didn't. However, there was one girl who was almost infatuated with me! Most days I wanted to be like, "GURL! Ugh! Stop talking to me!" But she would not leave me alone. We were opposites. While I was being a grumpy face, she was my ray of sunshine. My Sandy! She was a year or two older than me.

At our first encounter, her face lit up like a Christmas tree. I didn't know what she was so happy about, but I put a fake smile on my face too. She introduced herself and then I found out why she was *so* happy. She was a new mom. We *all* know how new moms go on and on about their new bundle of joy. They want to tell anyone who is willing to listen to what their lil' baby is doing every minute of the day at every moment. *Lord, help me!* It's what I thought many days, but there was something inside of me that kind of looked forward to seeing her and hoped that she was scheduled to work the same days I was. It could be because when we worked the same shift, she always wanted to feed me. She would buy me ice cream. I was a sucker for sweet treats. So, I gladly obliged when she offered to take me on a sweet treats break.

I listened to her never-ending stories about how she enjoyed being pregnant. *Well, can you be pregnant for me?* She kept going about how she loved her baby girl; she even told me that I was going to love my baby girl.

Whoa, whoa, whoa! Listen, baby girl, I don't even want this baby girl. So, I am not gonna be as elated and overjoyed as you are.

I never revealed that to her because I was too embarrassed to say it. I would just smile, eat my ice cream and listen to her talk. The funny thing was that she was the only one who genuinely appeared happy for me. She smiled when she asked how I was doing. She beamed with joy when she shared memories of her pregnancy. In fact, she always smiled and encouraged me, but she did not realize that's what she was doing. At the time, I didn't even know that she was encouraging me. But God knew and He used her to show me that He was still with me. He was extending His Grace to me.

My co-worker was the only one who intentionally acknowledged that I was pregnant. She wanted to know how I was doing and how the baby was doing. For whatever reason, she genuinely cared and was excited for me as if she was having a baby all over again! That type of support was necessary, and I didn't even know it at the time.

God uses others to bring hope into your situation; He is amazing like that. He used her to bring me a little bit of hope. Somewhere inside of me, a piece of me longed to smile. I wanted to genuinely smile again. However, each time I left her presence, I still struggled. I would go home and sit in my room alone. Although my family was there, I still felt alone. It was impossible for me to find the same excitement that my co-worker felt when she carried her daughter. It was because I didn't want to be a mom. I wanted to just be a college student and not have to deal with a plan b.

*~Access to His Grace~*

**Therefore encourage one another and build each other up, just as in fact you are doing.
—1 Thessalonians 5:11**

# Church Girls Apologize

Since I was raised in the church, I still gathered the courage to go to church every Sunday. Most Sundays I sat in the back of the sanctuary. Before I was pregnant, I sang in the church choir. I didn't want my belly to be on display, so I opted to sit in the general congregation while I was pregnant. A part of me didn't desire to go to church at all. I was disappointed in myself and although I wasn't mad at God, He wasn't top rank on my list of faves either. Even through all that I was dealing with, something inside of me nudged at me to lean into Him somehow. If I was going to trudge through my pregnancy without harming myself or the baby, I knew only He would be able to comfort me and convince me to stay the course. I needed God to show up for me so I could brag on Him as the old folks at church did. I needed Him to calm my fears and let me know that the physical detour was also part of a spiritual detour I had to take to birth His purpose in life.

As much as I needed to rely on God for His strength during my pregnancy, relying on His people was another story. I spent my adolescent and teenage years in the same church. There were many single mothers there so I would have been in great company once I delivered mine. As a matter of fact, there was another young lady my age that was pregnant with me. Yet, with all the unwed mothers in the place, never once had I witnessed what happened to me happen to anyone else.

It was a normal Sunday, church as usual. The choir sang some spirit rousing anthems, and the preacher preached a lengthy sermon with hundreds of amens following. It was a typical Baptist service until it wasn't typical anymore. Something weird and unexpected happened. The pastor called me to the front of the church. *Well, why? What have I done? I have been coming to church, me and my stomach minding our own business. I don't have anything to say. Why am I being called to the front of the church?*

With hesitation and confusion, I walked to the front of the church. Deep down inside, I wanted to ball my eyes out. I wasn't sure what was going on, but I knew it couldn't be good. And low and behold, it wasn't good at all. It was horrific! The pastor thought it would be in my best interest to stand before the church and apologize. *Oh my God! Apologize to who? And what the hell for?! Surely, Jesus didn't tell you to make me do this? And if He did, could He have consulted with me first? Gave me some warning? Did my family know he had this plan? If so, it would've been nice for them to have had a conversation with me.*

I was so humiliated and felt betrayed and angry! I stood before the church, my family and the pastor and repeated every word that he said as I held back tears.

"I have sinned. Please forgive me for my sin."

I focused more on holding back tears than the words that were coming out of my mouth. I was in such disbelief. It seemed like the world stopped as I stood in front of the congregation repeating these words that I did not understand. I did not understand why the more I tried to hide, the more attention I received. It was not only humiliating, but it was frustrating. It was like my mistake was never going to be forgiven and more so, never forgotten.

Once I finished "my pastor's" apology "to God," I went back to my seat and didn't say a word to anyone. I wish I could've just run away and never returned. When church was over, I did my best to put on my poker face and pretend like everything was okay -- that it was normal, like I wasn't exposed and humiliated in front of the church that I was born and raised in. The same church that became my family. I thought that family was supposed to protect you. I felt betrayed by my biological family and my church family. The families that were supposed to shield and protect me from the outside world. Nope! My family did not protect me at church and never said anything, not even at home. It was like it didn't happen. Just like me having a baby wasn't happening.

We did not discuss my pregnancy at home. We just moved around my belly. I didn't want to be noticed but I know they noticed my belly as it was growing just like my sister's was. My nephew definitely noticed though. Once after my niece was born. My sister was changing my niece on our mother's bed, and she was doing what she did best, crying. My nephew said very casually, "tete having a baby too." My sister looked at me and said with a slight chuckle, "well yea she is. I guess we haven't said anything." You guess, honey, no we haven't said anything, and I was OK with that. We didn't know what to say. None of us really did. We were all just trying to get through this moment to see what the future held for me and my baby.

It was somewhat of an advantage and disadvantage that my sister was pregnant at the same time too. No one talked about my pregnancy; they only spoke about hers. She got the smiles and the elevated voices when they saw her stomach. I got the frowns, the looks of disappointment and the oh you're pregnant too fake smile but let me change the subject as quickly as possible, look when they looked at my belly. Bold people even had the audacity to say, "I am so disappointed in you." and "I didn't expect you to ever be pregnant." Well, looka there, me neither!

As time progressed, it became natural for me to hold my head down and avoid eye contact anytime someone looked my way. I just wanted to disappear. Every single day I wanted to disappear. However, as much as I wanted to disappear, I never had the urge to commit suicide. There was something inside keeping me from committing suicide or even having suicidal thoughts. Something that helped me get out of bed every day and do life. Although I cried every day, sometimes multiple times a day, I still pushed through.

**You are my hiding place; you will protect me from trouble and surround me with songs of deliverance.**

—**Psalm 32:7**

# Don't Shower Me

My friends at the time threw me a small baby shower in my mom's basement. The funny thing is that I can't remember all the details of the baby shower. Partly because I don't want to remember. That was not how I pictured my life at eighteen. That was not how I pictured my baby shower. But what I do recall is that I absolutely did not want to be there.

My older cousin insisted on throwing me a baby shower. I refused because I didn't want to be on display. I couldn't understand what people didn't understand. I was not a proud, pregnant woman. I was ashamed. I was hurt and felt defeated. Nevertheless, my friends were persistent and wouldn't take 'no' for an answer. I had no energy to fight. So, they planned a shower in which I had no input.

During the baby shower, my mom, sister, and other mother (the name I gave my daughter's paternal grandmother) were upstairs in the kitchen doing whatever they were doing. They never once came downstairs. My sister didn't attend because she didn't believe in baby showers for unwed mothers. My mom--I honestly don't know. Maybe she was disappointed that I was pregnant, about to have a baby and not away on a college campus. And my other mother, well, she just chose to extend her moral support from the kitchen table because she never came down to mingle at the shower either.

It was just a few friends, my daughter's dad, his friends, and my belly. My vision of my first baby shower certainly looked nothing like that. I didn't want to be in that basement having a celebration. I don't even reminisce on that day. It's one of the many days I've since blocked out of my mind. I would have rather been comparing my first semester with my friends' college experience. My mind longed to laugh about how my roommate and I don't get along and how I would be choosing a new one next semester. Or perhaps daydream about my campus crush. The one in my English 101 class. Who was super cute, tall, and walked like a ballplayer. Mmmhmm... But no! That was all a dream deferred that I continued to pray was a nightmare and I'd wake up and shake it off. But it wasn't. I was living in my reality at that moment. In the basement of my mom's house with cake, balloons and a handful of people, my reality was that I would soon be called mom.

**Even though I walk through the darkest valley, I will fear no evil, for you are with me; your rod and your staff, they comfort me.**
**—Psalm 23:4**

# Why Do Women Do This?

On Friday, December 29, 2000, it all began; I went into labor. I didn't know at first until I made it to what would be my last doctor's appointment. In my wheat-colored Nike boots, I trudged through the snow to my final exam. The appointment began with the normal check-up. My doctor explained that I was dilated two centimeters. He further explained that I could be two centimeters for a while since my due date wasn't until January 5, 2001.

*Sooo, Doctor, what you're saying is that I'm just walking around, open?*

I was confused.

*And this is why I don't need to have a baby.*

I was confused about the whole centimeter process and the scary part was he said I could be open like that for a while before the baby came. Well, he was wrong. Little baby was ready! The next time I saw my doctor, my legs were spread wide open.

My bedroom still wasn't quite ready for the arrival of my little baby. And since I wasn't sure if lil' baby was on her way or not, I needed to quickly finish turning my bedroom into *our* bedroom. We had a crib and a dresser for her, but I still needed to make space for her tiny clothes in my closet.

The next day, Sat. December 30, 2000, I wobbled to The Container Store to pick up the last of the closet materials for our shared closet. The entire time while at the store , I was contracting. Contracting and scared. That was it. I would be a mother sooner than later.

After two days of being in labor and thinking God was punishing me with those indescribable labor pains, I thought my body was breaking in half!

*How do women do this over and over? My body could never ever get used to THIS type of pain.*

Good Lord, I thought I was gonna die and not make it!
*The death angels are coming to get me.*

Interestingly, I've learned that's how life is. When we go through valleys, we think, 'This is unbearable' or 'This hurts.' We even question God, "Why is this pain so great?" "Why do I have to go through this," and "Will I make it?" Yet, we always do. We make it and look back and say, "It was nothing but God's grace that carried me through."

I didn't see it at that moment though. In fact, I didn't see it for a few years. I couldn't smile right away at my blessing because I was still dealing with the pain. Although the physical pain ended after my daughter arrived, the mental pain remained for years to come.

**Even though I walk through the darkest valley, I will fear no evil, for you are with me; your rod and your staff, they comfort me.**
**—Psalm 23:4**

# Medicating the Pain of My Guilt

On New Year's Eve of 2000, at 3:54pm, I delivered an 8lb 4oz baby girl. I was surprised she came out over eight pounds the way I was squeezing my stomach for hours at a time when I first found out that I was pregnant! My first gift to her, after life, of course, was her name. Zharia Aianna Woods, who we affectionately nicknamed ZZ. Zharia means princess in Hebrew and little flower in Arabic. During the last days of my pregnancy, my mom surprised me one day and asked could she give Zharia her middle name. Not wanting any more smoke, I said yes without any hesitation or thought. Afterward, I was praying that the name wasn't something from the '50s like Judith or Magdalene. She did well though! She asked me if she could name her after the woman in the Bible named Anna, who was a prophet. Her variation was Aianna. I was very grateful, and I loved the name as well as the story behind the name. In my hospital room, I searched for answers on how any of it was possible. I mean, just six months prior, I had just graduated from high school. Six months later and I was a mother. How Sway, how? Reality hit fast when I stared at my glossy, brown-eyed baby in the face.

The night after I delivered my baby, I laid in the hospital bed alone staring deep into those eyes. My tear ducts opened for what seemed like the millionth time, but that time I cried for so many reasons. I didn't think I'd be a good enough mom. I didn't know how to parent. I didn't know how to soothe the baby when she cried. How would I know what she wanted? Would I be able to meet her needs? I didn't have any money except for my school refund checks and a little money saved from my Marshall Field's job.

Somewhere in my mind, I knew she was a blessing, but I just couldn't accept my blessing. At least not right at that moment. I wanted to accept her in another fifteen years or so. I know that sounds crazy, but I always imagined that I would become a mom around the age of 35 (really 37 because I was good with being an Advanced Maternal Age mom). I imagined myself married to a basketball player (don't judge me; you have heard me say it already), owning a home and *then* having a baby. Not having a baby, having a baby daddy, and still living at home with my mom. That was not in my "what do you want to be when you grow up?" speech.

On the afternoon I was slated to name my baby, I was hesitant. I was hesitant not because I thought Zharia Aianna wasn't the perfect name. I was hesitant because I didn't want to give my daughter her father's last name. I know to some that may sound crazy or mean. He was her dad but because we weren't married, I didn't think giving her his last name was in either of our best interests. *Our* meaning baby girl and me.

When it was determined that we were keeping the baby, I discussed this name issue with her dad. He petitioned that he wanted the baby to take his last name, but I was leery. I understood that if my daughter and I had different last names, it would further perpetuate the fact that I was a young, unwed mother, aka a baby mama.

Ultimately, I caved the day we officially gave baby girl her name. It came with much hesitation though. As I recited the name that would officially be baby girl's forever—*Zharia Aianna...*

I paused and looked over at her dad who appeared desperate for his daughter to share his name. So, I gave her his last name.

*~Access to His Grace~*

When the nurses came around to ask if I wanted ZZ to go to the nursery, I declined. I just wanted to stare at her. Surprisingly, I wanted to get to know her.

The nurses were so nurturing and accommodating. They were not only concerned about ZZ, but they were concerned about me. In some strange but comforting way, I enjoyed being at the hospital. A part of me didn't want to go home. So, when asked if I felt like I needed to stay another day, I gladly obliged. But eventually, my fantasy life ended, and I had to go home.

On the day Zharia and I were slated to go home together, I gently slid into a wheelchair that was rolled in for me. Once I was situated, the nurse handed me Zharia. I'm not sure why but I asked the nurse to give Zharia to her dad and she nicely explained that only the mother could hold the baby as we exited the hospital. As I held ZZ in my arms while being rolled out to Brother-dad's car, I whispered to myself, "Don't cry again. It's going to be ok." It was like I was rolling into a dream because I had no idea if it really was going to be ok.

Please understand that I loved my baby. I loved her with a mother's love, but there was still something inside of me that earnestly fought motherhood. I wanted to be *her* mom, not just *a* mom. Honestly, I always feared that God would take her away from me because I didn't appreciate her. I couldn't see my blessing and accept the grace that He extended to me. The guilt weighed on me day and night and I did what anyone would do who wanted it all to stop. I developed an addiction. I shopped and shopped and shopped. Now I know you may be thinking that shopping is not such a bad habit to have. It's called retail therapy, right? We all do it. No, it was an addiction and I truly understand it could've been worse. I could have turned to alcohol or drugs. But again, God extended His grace.

I used shopping to suppress my thoughts of guilt, anger, and shame. I was in my happy place while I shopped just as a heroin addict is in her happy place after that hit she's been feening for since the last hit. From Louis Vuitton all the way down to Gap, I was on a high. I shopped for me, and I shopped for ZZ. She was so cute. Basically, a walking GAP ad. I dressed my issue up. Dressing her up made it appear to the outside world that we were perfect. It look like I had dealt with the pain of my disappointment. But I really hadn't. We have all dressed our issues up. We dress the part.

No one could see my hurting soul because my baby stayed dressed in the latest. She appeared to be very well taken care of. From matching headbands and bows down to fancy tights and ruffled socks. My issue was all in disguise covering my uncertainty, guilt, and shame.

*~Access to His Grace~*

The first year was tough. It was time to let go of the "what if's" and "if I didn't have a child" because the reality was that I had a child, and she wasn't going anywhere. It's not like I really wanted her to leave because I did love her with all my heart, but I just wished I could love her later with my entire being. If I was better prepared mentally, I would have been so much better for her. Instead, I harbored feelings of guilt, despondency, and disappointment. The guilt stemmed from knowing that a child was a blessing and God could take her from me any moment for being ungrateful. The despondency was a result of living a life that I dreaded. My daily existence was a far cry from friends'. They lived normal college girls' lives. Lastly, the disappointment came from resenting my role as a single mom. I always said I would never be like my mom and be a single mom. I knew it wasn't something I wanted on my "resume", so I continued to refuse to accept the role. Because I refused to accept the role, I loved my daughter in hiding.

My new reality, the baby, stared me in my face daily and still, I was a far cry from the typical mom--whatever that is. I went from feeling nauseated from carrying a baby for nine months to feeling sick and nauseous every day that I wasn't away at college like I was supposed to be. I lived two lives. One as ZZ's mom and one as Kentavia, the college student. I was never Kentavia, Zharia's mom because I was too ashamed of that title. During the day, I acted as if she didn't exist. I went to my college classes every day as if I was a traditional college student who just lived off campus. After school, I hung out with my friends. Sure, there were other girls who had babies. I knew because they talked about their babies. Meanwhile, I didn't make any mention of my baby. I never spoke about ZZ. Instead, I made a conscious decision to talk about fashion, music, classes, parties, and TV. No stories about my baby's new teeth, first steps or babble words. Now, if I didn't mention her name, it's a no-brainer that I never showed any pictures of her. If I started gloating about her, I knew that I would begin to feel like a mother. I couldn't let myself slip like that. Therefore, I had blocked my feelings by not talking about it. All I wanted was to feel like the person I had always envisioned myself to be--an accomplished college student.

As crazy as it sounds, even after giving birth to my daughter and loving her with a mother's love, I still could not wholeheartedly accept and embrace my role. Something inside of me was still preventing me from freely walking in my role. I was still reduced to tears at the thought of how my life turned out, only I had two things to blame at that point. One, because I wanted to be my ZZ's mom but not *a* mom, and two, because I was afraid that since I refused to accept my role as a mother, God would take her away from me. I never wanted God to take her away from me; I just didn't want her at that moment. My greatest wish would have been to just put her on the shelf for later. I would come back and get her when I was ready.

*Right now, I'm just not ready. I don't know how to be a mother.*

Mentally, I just wasn't there. My mind was ready for the next college party, watching the season finale of American Idol or cram studying all night for midterms and finals. Yet, my body was changing pampers and soothing a newborn's cries.

Have you ever been in a place and you felt so alone as though no one understood you or how you felt? That is exactly where I found myself residing. Who could I call and say, "I love my baby, but I don't want my baby?" In my mind, no one could relate to that. I had heard no one express such a disgraceful truth. So, I continued to hold my ugly truth deep inside. I suppressed it enough to carry out the basic functions of motherhood. Other than that, I just kept crying and living two separate lives.

**The Lord has heard my cry for mercy; the Lord accepts my prayer.
—Psalm 6:9**

# It's Not Your Fault, Baby

Zharia was the perfect baby. Her skin was chocolate brown accented by her beautifully round, intriguing eyes and a smile that would make even the grumpiest old lady smile back. Not only was she gorgeous, but she was such a good baby too. Zharia slept well at night and only cried when necessary. Even when she was cutting her first tooth, she did not carry on like I see other babies do...a.k.a. my niece! I think God knew—no, I KNOW God knew that if ZZ had my niece's temperament, I would have possibly thrown myself out the window.

Overall, Zharia was just a chill baby. Most days, ZZ entertained herself if she was in a playful mood. She would even soothe herself in the rare instances that she was upset. While I did my homework, she would lay across her Boppy pillow and either suck her bottle or play quietly with her fingers. Now that I reflect on how detached I was, that was possibly one of her learned survival tactics.

As she grew older, I noticed a certain behavior. I know it was only God who revealed it to me. Around the age of three, I noticed she would hold her head down whenever anyone talked to her. My baby was carrying *my* shame. The same shame that I held close to my heart the entire time that I carried her in my womb. She was a quiet child so to the outside world, it may have been mistaken as shyness, but a mother knows when something is wrong with their child. I knew that she was struggling with her esteem, finding her voice and confidence even at an early age. I knew that I had planted those seeds of rejection and shame in her long before she knew me as her mother. I knew that it wasn't her fault, and she was going to need some help digging her way out of that mess. I knew that it was a mess that I created and the only way that I was going to help my baby was to help myself. So, for seven years, I went to war for my baby and for myself. I adamantly fought to save her, to save our mother-daughter relationship and to save me.

Day and night, I cried out to God and searched the Bible for scriptures to ease my pain. I needed scriptures to save my baby from the enemy's evil, sneaky plan. I had to find words in the good book that would quiet the awful words of, "well, see if you didn't have this baby, then you could…" or "your life would be good if you didn't have to take care of this baby…" Those lies haunted me during my quiet times and I needed something to silence them once and for all. I searched the Bible for strength and the truth about who I was. I wanted to know God's promises for both my baby and me. I was determined to find scriptures to give me the strength to speak against anything coming against me.

**Finally, be strong in the Lord and in his mighty power. Put on the full armor of God, so that you can take your stand against the devil's schemes. Ephesians 6:10-11 NIV**

I know this may sound cliché, but I made it through that storm with word, worship, and prayer.

**Therefore, since we have been justified through faith, we have peace with God through our Lord Jesus Christ, through whom we have gained access by faith into this grace in which we now stand. And we boast in the hope of the glory of God. Not only so, but we also glory in our sufferings, because we know that suffering produces perseverance; perseverance, character; and character, hope. And hope does not put us to shame, because God's love has been poured out into our hearts through the Holy Spirit, who has been given to us. You see, at just the right time, when we were still powerless, Christ died for the ungodly. Romans 5:1-6 NIV**

I recited this scripture over and over until I memorized it and it was embedded in my spirit. Anytime I came up against thoughts that did not align with where I wanted to be as a mom, I recited my scripture. I stood on this scripture for seven years until I had the courage to be a mom in private and public, to love and appreciate my baby in the present. To cherish every moment that we had together and never want to leave from that place. To nurture her and protect her all the days of her life.

During those seven years, I allowed myself to heal from the inside out. The healing allowed me to decree and declare that I would be able to take care of my baby all the days of her life. Healing would allow me to love being a mother and encourage other mothers to cherish motherhood as well no matter what circumstances their babies were born in.

# Access to His Grace

It amazes me when I see young girls who are pregnant or parenting babies or toddlers come into the high school where I work. I marvel at how they post pictures on social media standing with their child's father. In some ways, I envy them because they carry pride that I didn't have the strength to carry until seven years after the birth of my daughter. I wish I could have stood tall, with my head held high knowing that I may have sinned, but the blessing of my daughter was never meant to bring me condemnation, guilt, or shame.

Those three wardens kept me locked in a mental and emotional prison far too long. I cried every day during my pregnancy. Anytime I looked at my stomach and it was still there, I cried. I hoped to wake up to a miscarriage. I even once fell, and I prayed that I would just bleed out and the baby inside of me would die. My plan was to just move on with my life after that tragic day. But God!

God had a different plan. While it seemed like a major physical detour and distraction on the outside, it was the detour God wanted and needed me to take. The route changed what was necessary to birth purpose in my life. I birthed my daughter and through my struggles, I birthed the power to share my story to inspire and help others heal. That unexpected change of plans birthed the microphone which was prophesied that I would speak on. Here I am on my mic!

**Being confident of this, that he who began a good work in you will carry it on to completion until the day of Christ Jesus. Philippians 1:6**

In the Bible, Naomi and Ruth's lives took a detour. They were in a foreign land and experienced great loss. They lost their men whom they trusted and followed there. I imagine that they were grieving and feeling hopeless. Hence, Naomi told her daughters-in-law to go back to their mothers because she felt God had turned against her. It seems like Naomi may have been depressed and when we are depressed, we tend to isolate ourselves. We don't go outside, and we push the people away who are sent to help us. And that's exactly what Naomi did; she tried to push her daughters-in-law away. One took Naomi's suggestion and said, "Okay, peace out mother-in-law. Imma pray for you. You're right; I'm still young and tender. Let me go see what God has for me!"

But that other daughter-in-law, Ruth, was a G! She stayed and I'm sure she was scared and nervous, but there was something on the inside that pushed her. A small voice told her, "Eventually, Ruth, it's gonna be alright. What it looks like now will not be forever."

Their detour in life was just God's plan to get Ruth and Naomi to trust Him. He wanted them to trust His will for their life. As a result, I'm sure Ruth became wise. She trusted her mother-in-law when she gave her directions and, in the end, God showed Ruth favor.

In David Ramos' book, *Daring with Ruth*, he sums it up like this: "Profound pain, when placed in the hands of God, leads to profound opportunity. But only if we are willing." Basically, God eventually works things out for your good.

Don't begrudge the detours life may bring. God knows exactly what He is doing with every trouble and delay we face. Every detour is not a detriment. It may be God's way of showing you *the* way. God has already considered the detours, mistakes, and broken pieces of our lives so we must forgive ourselves and accept His mercy and grace. The key to fully opening up and accepting His grace and mercy is trusting His will for our lives. There is godly confidence that comes with knowing that you have access to His grace!

*****

For me to access God's grace that He genuinely extended, I had to start with forgiveness. I had to forgive myself. If I didn't, I wouldn't be able to be the mom my daughter needed me to be. If I didn't forgive myself, I wouldn't be able to be who God called me to be. I had to start with forgiving myself for becoming someone I didn't want to become – a single mom. It was so hard to utter those words. I was a mom. For some women, it comes so easy. They pray for the day when they are blessed to have children. After I genuinely decided to forgive myself, God showed me mothers who struggled to conceive. You may think that was mean, but it wasn't. It was God giving me access to His grace. He allowed my heart to become open to my blessing and my purpose. He used the pathway of my eyes and ears, to see and hear women talk passionately about their many miscarriages and how they hoped to become pregnant one day and experience motherhood. My heart began to ache for those women who wanted to become mothers more than anything in the world.

**Let all bitterness, and wrath, and anger, and clamour, and evil speaking, be put away from you, with all malice: 32 And be ye kind one to another, tenderhearted, forgiving one another, even as God for Christ's sake hath forgiven you. Ephesians 4:31-32**

This scripture sounds like, "oh ok, I'll just forgive. I'll say, I'm sorry and move on." It was definitely not that easy at all! I had to have the patience and strength to do what needed to be done.

I had to forgive my mom because to me she took away something that I so desperately wanted --to go away to college. Right where her firm 'no' stood, I erected a wall of distrust. I felt like she didn't trust me. Although she stated that her decision was for my safety, I didn't agree. I had made it *safely* six months with no prenatal care, carrying my secret and my shame to myself. I would have been just fine. For me, it only translated to her continuing not to trust me. That would be a strain in our relationship through adulthood. Thus, I had to make an intentional effort to forgive her so that I could fully access the grace and forgiveness that God was giving to me.

Finally, I had to ask God to forgive me. Forgive me, one, for sinning. As a church girl, of course, I know I sinned. Sex before marriage is a no-no. But also, for not trusting the process. For not trusting that my baby was supposed to be in this world at the moment He brought her here. For not trusting that my life and my baby's life was in His hand. For not trusting Him when He wrote my story. He knew who I needed and when I needed them. He knew when I needed my baby. I had to ask for forgiveness for trying to take my child's life. It wasn't about what others thought of me, it was what I thought of myself. I disappointed myself.

**Prayer:** *Thank You Lord that you are guiding my life and my story. Help me to trust You in every difficult season. Give me the confidence to know that you have specifically placed me where I'm at today to fulfill your purposes. In Jesus' Name, Amen!*

*It's Available to You*

Are you carrying the weight of your sins when God died to bear the weight? Are you carrying things that God's asked you to release? How much more are you going to take, when God just wants you to trust in him? What you believe about God's design and creation of you will affect your ability to trust and believe Him in every area of your life. I believe that my life was perfectly designed by God in every way! I affirm that all the intricate details that make me who I am—my body shape, my personality type, and my intellect—were purposefully woven together by Him. No matter what I have been taught, what has been said to me, or what sin I have committed, nothing can change the fact that God loves me and beautifully created me to bring Him glory! I believe those same things for you, too!

You may think that your circumstances or mistakes matter, but God's grace matters even more. It alone provides both the strength and the freedom we need. When God is our hiding place, no matter where we've been, what we've done, or who we are, we have access to forgiveness instead of guilt, grace instead of shame, confidence instead of fear, and hope instead of despair.

Don't become so discouraged in the delays that you give up on the pursuit of your purpose. Trust the process. The presence of difficulty is often God laying the foundation for his greater work to come true. God is developing you for the plan He has created you to live out. The God who works all things together for good will leverage every experience, every skill, every mistake, and every bit of knowledge you have acquired.

**I will give you hidden treasures, riches stored in secret places, so that you may know that I am the Lord, the God of Israel, who summons you by name. Isaiah 45:3**

In Mark Batterson's book, *Draw The Circle: The 40 Day Prayer Challenge,* he wrote, "we fail to learn the lessons God is trying to teach us or cultivate the character God is trying to grow in us because we're so focused on God changing the circumstances that we never allow God to change us! Change our hearts."

Fear robbed me of the life God planned for me. I can honestly say that I spent so much time wallowing in the pity of my circumstances, that I missed everything that God was trying to show me. He wanted me to know that I was not being punished; He was richly blessing me with a beautiful daughter. He wanted me to know that I did not have to stay locked in a self-inflicted cage of fear, guilt, shame, and condemnation. God desired for me to accept His word, His truth. The truth was the access to His grace was the key to unlock my freedom. It does not matter how terribly you think you messed up; that same freedom is available to you as well. Open up and accept His grace!

**Then you will know the truth, and the truth will set you free.**
**—John 8:32**

# Mother-Daughter Activity

It is my prayer that this book will strengthen the bonds between mothers and daughters. For that reason, I have included an activity for you to share with your own mother or daughter. The purpose is to help break down the walls that are sometimes knowingly and unknowingly erected between moms and their girls.

Daughters, take some time to ask your mother these questions. You will get a better understanding of who she is and possibly why she thinks or acts the way she does. This may even help you to better understand who you are as a woman. Mothers, although you may feel as if you know how your baby girl would respond, please feel free to throw the ball back into her court. Take a moment to listen to her. You may be surprised at how much you learn about her today.

*~Access to His Grace~*

1. Have you ever been heartbroken ? If so, how did you handle it?
2. Is there something you regret not doing?
3. Did having children hinder achieving your goals?
4. Have you ever questioned God?
5. What do you do when your faith wavers?
6. What did you want to be when you grew up?
7. What makes you afraid?
8. What things are most important to you?
9. When you were younger, did you have a crush?
10. Why did you choose to be with my dad?
11. As a child, what did you enjoy doing?
12. What accomplishment are you most proud of?
13. What do you do when you are mistreated?
14. What is the most rewarding about having children?
15. How was your relationship with your parents?
16. Tell me about the day I was born.
17. What advice would you give about dating and marriage?
18. Is there someone from your past that you still think about?
19. Have you ever had a fight?
20. How did you handle an argument with a close friend?

*~Access to His Grace~*

By profession, Kentavia Johnson is an educator who works specifically with the special education population. Her work with adolescents and teens has afforded her the opportunity to develop a love for young people. As a mother, Kentavia has learned the meaning of grace at work in her life.

She is the mother of a college student and her journey to acceptance of motherhood is uncanny. Using her story of guilt, shame and rejection, Kentavia encourages other women who find themselves resenting their pregnancies and children because it did not happen the way they thought it would.

Even though her topics may be heavy, Kentavia brings her humor and quick wit to any stage that she graces.

Born and raised in Chicago, Kentavia enjoys spending quality time with her daughter and close friends and family. She is also an avid baker, and you can find her regularly trying new yummy recipes.

www.ingramcontent.com/pod-product-compliance
Lightning Source LLC
Chambersburg PA
CBHW070050120526
44589CB00034B/1685